A Note to Parents

Read to your child...

★ Reading aloud is one of the best ways to develop your child's love of reading. Older readers still love to hear stories.

★ Laughter is contagious. Read with feeling. Show your child that reading is fun.

★ Take time to answer questions your child may have about the story. Linger over pages that interest your child.

...and your child will read to you.

★ Do not correct every word your child misreads.
Say, "Does that make sense? Let's try it again."

★ Praise your child as he progresses. Your encouraging words will build his confidence.

You can help your Level 2 reader.

★ Keep the reading experience interactive. Read part of a sentence, then ask your child to add the missing word.

★ Read the first part of a story, then ask your child, "What's going to happen next?"

★ Give clues to new words. Say, "This word begins with *b* and ends in *ake*, like *rake, take, lake*."

★ Ask your child to retell the story using her own words.

★ Use the five *W*s: WHO is the story about? WHAT happens? WHERE and WHEN does the story take place? WHY does it turn out the way it does?

Most of all, enjoy your reading time together!

Photo credits: Front cover, page 6, page 22, page 26 ©2004 Action Sports Photography, Inc.;
title page, page 4, 5, 9, 10, 11, 12, 13, 14, 16, 19, 21, 27, 30, 31 ©2004 Sherryl Creekmore/NASCAR;
page 7, page 18, page 20, page 24, page 29 CIA Stock Photography, Inc.

Library of Congress Cataloging-in-Publication Data

Kelley, K.C.
Daring drivers : if you were a NASCAR driver / by K.C. Kelley.
      p. cm — (All-star readers. Level 2)
ISBN 0-7944-0602-5
[1. Stock car drivers—Juvenile literature. 2. Stock car drivers—pictorial works—Juvenile
literature.] I. Title. II. All-star readers. Level 2.

GV1029.9.S74K45 2004 796.72—dc 22   2004053175

Daring Drivers

If You Were a NASCAR Driver

by K.C. Kelley

All-Star Readers™

Reader's Digest Children's Books™

Pleasantville, New York • Montréal, Québec

A NASCAR driver has one of the coolest jobs in the world. He races fast cars on famous tracks. And he loves what he does.

But it's more than just fun. Being a driver is hard work, too. A driver's weekend at the track begins quietly. It ends in a burst of speed and noise. Imagine what it would be like if YOU were a NASCAR driver....

A busy weekend at the track begins. First, you'd arrive at the track in a giant motor home! The race is set for Sunday, so the race teams get to the track on Thursday to get ready.

Motor homes are like houses on wheels. A driver and his family live in one all weekend. It is nice to have a place to relax. Then it's time to get to work.

A driver's life is filled with action. He travels from track to track, testing his skills. But being a NASCAR driver is a job, not just fun.

If you were a driver, you'd meet with your team on Friday of a race weekend. NASCAR racing is a team sport. Many people help the drivers. Some work on the car and the engine. Others will help during the race.

Drivers have to follow NASCAR rules. Before every race, all cars are checked. Officials measure each car to make sure it's exactly the right size and shape. They check the engines, too. The drivers watch closely.

Later that day, it's time to drive—
fast! Drivers zoom around the
track at top speed for one lap. It's
called a qualifying lap. The fastest
drivers get the best starting spots
in the race.

Practice is what makes a good driver a great one. If you were a driver, on Saturday you'd drive practice laps on the track.

he teams watch the practice laps osely. Drivers check in with their ams on the radio. Together, they ill try to plan the perfect race.

NASCAR fans love to meet their favorite drivers. Drivers are stars! At each race, drivers meet fans and sign autographs. They also talk to writers and TV reporters.

Everyone wants to hear from the drivers! If you were a driver, talking with fans and TV crews would be another part of your job.

It's the morning of the race. In your motor home, you wake up with your family. You eat breakfast together. Then everyone heads to the garage.

Drivers and crews are not nervous on race day. They have worked hard all week. Now it is time to see if all the hard work will pay off.

If you were a driver, you would have to put on special clothes before the race. There are many pieces of safety gear you would wear. You would put on special underwear that would protect you from heat. Then you would put on a colorful, one-piece jumpsuit.

On your feet, you would wear special boots. You would also put on driving gloves. These would help you grip the steering wheel.

The stands have filled with fans. The cheering grows louder. Each driver's name is called. Drivers come out and wave to the fans. All the drivers and crews line up on pit row. They stand while the National Anthem is played.

The race is just moments away. It's time for you to climb into the car…through the window! NASCAR race cars don't have doors!

In the car, you put on one more
piece of safety gear—the helmet.
Drivers slip their helmets on their
heads carefully. They know how
important their helmets are.

Now the fans are roaring in the stands. But it's quiet in the car. You take a deep breath. *This is it,* you think. *This is where all the hard work pays off.*

You can feel the power of your car's mighty engine. The pace car leads the cars onto the track. Each driver follows the car in front of his own. The 43 cars cruise around the track for a few laps.

The green flag drops! If you're a driver, you stomp on the gas pedal. Suddenly, you're racing at top speed! The wind whips in through the window! The noise is incredible!

For the next three hours, a driver must pay attention every second. The cars are sometimes just inches apart from each other. Your eyes scan the track ahead. You look for any chance to pass other cars.

The race teams help their drivers with superfast pit stops. They give each car new tires and more gas. Then the cars zoom back to the race.

On the track, you see the leaders ahead. There are just a few laps to go. It's time to make your move. On the last lap, you see your chance—*ZOOM*—your car races into the lead!

Seconds later, the checkered flag drops…above your car! You won the race! You and your team's hard work has paid off!

The crew is excited, too.
Everyone jumps for joy! Now it's
time to head for Victory Lane.

Imagine what that would be like. You're celebrating with your team. You're holding up a shiny trophy. Your fans are cheering for you. It feels great! You're a winning NASCAR driver!

Words are fun!

Here are some simple activities you can do with a pencil, crayons, and a sheet of paper. You'll find the answers at the bottom of the page.

———— ★ ————

1. Pick the two words in each line that rhyme

> **track   back   truck**
>
> **near   fair   steer**
>
> **driver   river   shiver**
>
> **crews   crown   use**
>
> **wear   hear   care**

2. Imagine you are a NASCAR driver. Draw a picture of yourself wearing driver gear.

3. Find three things on this list that drivers do not do in this story:

> **race   talk   win**
>
> **drive   dance   hike**
>
> **swim   travel**

4. Can you remember which activity the driver does during the four days of a NASCAR race? Match the action with the correct day of the week.

> **a. Drive in the race**
>
> **b. Drive practice laps**
>
> **c. Arrive at the track**
>
> **d. Meet with the team**

Thursday _____

Friday _____

Saturday _____

Sunday _____